Al Cockrell has written a devotional where after 21 days you wished his pen had not stopped. He illustrates to us beautifully that because of the Cross, Jesus' wounds are our healings, His sufferings are our songs, and His death is our life. Thank You Pastor for reminding us of the powerful words of Watchmen Nee... "a long-lasting victory can never be separated from a long-lasting stand on the foundation of the cross."

Dr. Ken Whitten
Senior Pastor Idlewild Baptist Church

I had the God Ordained privilege of worshipping and learning under Dr. Cockrell's leadership, receiving first hand these 21 facts for life. Mandates of real hope, challenge, promise and Eternity. Twenty one, just as there are Epistles amidst the Gospels, to engage more fully the significance of Jesus' death and life. In this wonderful book, Al Cockrell has galvanized the reality of the Cross of Christ, once embedded at Golgotha but forever, lifting from bedrock to the only "rock" ... a "Living Stone."

D1158810

Al Cockrell's selfless and passionate heart impacted my life personally and professionally as I watched him live these realities. They are now beautifully and permanently penned for you and me as we celebrate God's Greatest Gift, Jesus.

Rev. Richard S. De Witt, past President and COO of
Marketplace Ministries, Inc.,
Lt. Col. USAFR Ret. and former businessman

I appreciate how Al Cockrell takes us straight to the cross in this twenty one day devotion, not a sanitized, Sunday school version of the cross, but rather the historical , atoning and yes, bloody cross. He masterfully captures the depth of suffering our Lord bore and yet the resurrection is never far away.

I stopped several times while reading to clear my mind as I pictured the graphic nature of what truly happened both relationally between the Father and the Son as well as the physical descriptions of the cross. You will be challenged, encouraged and stirred as you spend 21 days at the cross.

Rev. Paul Davis
President of ABWE, a mission agency of over one
thousand missionaries worldwide.

21 Days at the

CROSS

21 Days at the CROSS

ALAN COCKRELL

XULON PRESS

Xulon Press
2301 Lucien Way #415
Maitland, FL 32751
407.339.4217
www.xulonpress.com

Unless otherwise indicated, Scripture quotations taken from the Holy Bible, New International Version (NIV). Copyright © 1973, 1978, 1984, 2011 by Biblica, Inc.™. Used by permission. All rights reserved.

Printed in the United States of America.

ISBN-13: 978-1-6312-9136-4

DEDICATION

I want to dedicate this book to my best friend Janie, the love of my life for what will soon be 59 years of marriage. Though joined in marriage in 1961 it was not until 1964 that we became actively engaged as volunteer youth leaders in a young start-up church. From that moment to this she has not only been a loving wife, a trusted companion, the mother of our three wonderful sons, all of whom are in some form of ministry helping people, she has been a full partner in my call to ministry by making my call her passion as well.

Janie is one of the most ardent soul winners I know, having introduced countless numbers to the saving knowledge of Jesus Christ. She has not let up in her senior years as a trail of recent converts, many of those in their seventies, will attest too. She has consistently lifted the banner of the Cross of Jesus Christ, both by her words and by her life through these many years.

For me personally she has been my "completer", a term I believe describes her role as a "helpmeet" to me in ministry. Whatever successes I may have experienced as a pastor she shares as a faithful wife enthusiastically committed to the ministry. She has been willing to go anywhere, endure any hardship, move multiple times, all the while maintaining her love for me even when I least deserved it.

Over the two years of my writing and re-writing "21 Days At The Cross" Janie has been a constant source of encouragement believing in me as a writer though my writing previously was pretty much limited to writing sermons.

For all this Janie, I thank you and dedicate this book of devotions to you for I know your desire is to only boast "in the cross of our Lord Jesus Christ". (Galatians 6:14 ESV)

FOREWORD

Al Cockrell has done the body of Christ a great service. He has given us a 21-day journey in taking a fresh new look at the cross. It is amazing the number of songs that are written about the cross and about Good Friday. We will soon enter the Passion Week where all attention will be on Friday; where the ultimate was paid by Almighty God himself as He clothed Himself in flesh, lived a perfect life after coming into this world through a virgin birth in order to die on the cross.

I am grateful that on the cross the Lord Jesus absorbed the wrath that I deserved. I do not want to take for granted to have a single view and that be the compass and focus of all that I can see in the cross. In this 21-day journey you will take a different look, a different angle, a different focus, a different appreciation, a deeper love for the Lord Jesus and what he accomplished at the cross.

What Jesus did at the cross takes us back to the book of Genesis and finds its conclusion in the book of Revelation. It is the theme of God's Word; the truth is, it is something God did before the foundation of the world. It is amazing the territory that is covered throughout the Word of God and even human history when we think about the cross.

I pray that as you join me and thousands of others in taking a fresh new look daily at the cross of the Lord Jesus that your heart would be strangely warmed. I pray that as I embrace the cross it will remind me that the gospel is the power of God onto salvation. It is spelled out so clearly in 1 Corinthians 15 especially in verses three and four where the Apostle Paul reminds us that Jesus Christ died for our sins, that He was buried and thank God on the third day He rose from the dead, according to the Scriptures. This is the gospel and the gospel is for everyone. Every person that has ever breathed a breath of life. What Jesus did on the cross He did for them. But we know it is not realized in an individual's life until they embrace the cross through repentance of sin, receiving Christ as their Lord and Savior and then receiving the marvelous gift of eternal life.

May the cross be more real as a result of this writing, your reading, your embracing and your assimilating of this truth. May all of us thank Al Cockrell for helping us to love the cross even more.

Johnny Hunt

Senior Vice President, Evangelism/Leadership, North American Mission Board

Former President, Southern Baptist Convention

Former Senior Pastor, First Baptist Church Woodstock, GA

INTRODUCTION

Though these 21 realities of the cross do not capture all of its elaborate features, these are the ones which rolled off my pen during what seemed to me to be a burning in my soul for a fresh love of the Cross. Although they came to me in a matter of a few minutes, the features of each one I have now written about in this twenty-one-day devotion have been thirteen years in the making. I have always thought these twenty-one touch-stones of the cross should be placed in the hands of many, not because they are *my* creations, but because they came from God refreshing my heart with the wonderful features of the cross. When I first penned the words of "The Cross," I was preparing a message to preach, but it seems as though God was the one preaching to me and expanding my soul in order to be captured anew with the blessedness of the cross.

In June of 2005, the church where I was pastoring was about to celebrate the first service in its new facility. It was by all comparisons the largest building project of my forty-five years of ministry. The history of other projects had taught me how new facilities for a church family are not always easy to navigate. Sometimes pride gets in the way, and at other times disappointment is experienced by those who have a long history with the church when, at least in their minds, the new facility does not provide the intimacy the old facilities afforded. Others were so impressed by the new facility that they missed the point of why it was built in the first place.

With those and other thoughts as a backdrop, it was not just important but vital for the first service to be less about the *facility* and expressly more about the *facilitator*, Jesus. For all my ministry years, I have always believed nothing reveals the person of Jesus Christ as does the cross. When the veil, which concealed the Most Holy Place within the temple walls, was ripped from top to bottom at Christ's dying moment, He allowed God's glory to be seen in a most spectacular and specific manner.

Previously, only the Jewish high priest dared enter The Most Holy Place wherein dwelt the presence and glory of God represented by the ark of the covenant. His entrance was allowed only after much preparation had taken place, which included the offering of an animal sacrifice for the purpose of sprinkling its blood on the mercy seat. Even at that, the blood of sacrificial animals did not have lasting effect concerning the sins of man. When Jesus shed His blood, it not only opened the door for potentially the entire world to see the glory of God, but it eliminated the necessity of ever again offering any kind of animal sacrifice. From the moment Jesus shed his blood on the cross, the relationship initiated by faith between man and God became permanent. The apostle Paul was so taken by the magnificence of the cross he said, "But God forbid that I should glory, save in the cross of our Lord Jesus Christ, by whom the world is crucified unto me, and I unto the world" (Gal 6:14).

My hope is that it can be said that while in my ministry, although I'm sure had many flaws, I never lost sight of the centerpiece of history, the cross, and kept it the bedrock of my preaching. Some great sage of bygone years has been quoted as saying, "One can find the cross on every page of the Bible." I am not doubting this is true, but I will be the first to admit I have not found them all. What I have found is the longer I live the more the cross keeps showing up. In my lifetime I may never see the cross on every page, but new discoveries cause me to believe what the old sage said is true. His devout life simply allowed him to see what most do not, including me.

The following page contains the original statements about the Cross that the author first penned in June of 2005. A copy of the original is now on display in the homes of many of Al Cockrell's close friends.

THE CROSS

Heaven's most precious treasure was hung there.
Earth's greatest victory was won there.
Man's greatest enemy was defeated there.
The windows of hope were raised there.
The door of deliverance was opened there.
Oceans of grace were exposed there.
The greatest kindness was shown there.
Rivers of mercy were released there.
Fountains of cleansing burst forth there.
Mountains of opportunity began there.
Our strength is renewed there.
The greatest of friendships was initiated there.
The apex of forgiveness was reached there.
Man's peace with God was established there.
All of God's benefits were distributed.
The foundation stone of joy was laid there.
All our iniquities were nailed there.
Our redemption was purchased there.
The love of God was expressed there.
Our robe of righteousness was woven there.
The search for satisfaction ends there.

HEAVEN'S MOST PRECIOUS TREASURE WAS HUNG THERE

B efore there were artists such as Eakins, Rembrandt, Grunewald, and a myriad of others who sought to depict the crucifixion of Christ, God the Father already had a picture of this unparalleled event captured in His mind. Before our world was even created, in His foreknowledge God knew there would be a place called Golgotha where His only Son would hang upon a cross. Before the event took place, God the Father knew what the moment would look like when His and heaven's most precious treasure would be nailed to the tree. As fallen, earthly parents we can still understand the immense value of our children; how much more perfectly does the Heavenly Father comprehend the value, the treasure, that was His only son, Jesus?

While it is impossible to know for sure what was happening in heaven at the moment of the crucifixion, we can certainly imagine. Angels may have folded their wings. Michael and Gabriel possibly stood at a loss for words, having never felt the pain of sin personally, only to now hear the Son of God call out in agony to his

Father, referring to Him instead in a far less personal way "My God" (Matt. 27:46). Did God cry in grief over his most precious son dying alone and without him? It's impossible to know for sure. We know He did in His human form when Jesus wept over the death of his close friend Lazarus (John 11:35 NIV). Did the angels witness the Heavenly Father shedding tears over his son? Our human emotions seem to demand it, though we cannot know for sure.

While the pain experienced by the Father in heaven is beyond our human ability to grasp, we can get a glimpse of how greatly the Savior was treasured in heaven by looking at the unprecedented celebration and welcoming home that took place after his resurrection from the grave. Read the description in Psalm 24 when the "King of Glory" returns to heaven. Although it is impossible to capture what the scene in heaven was like, when you consider a soldier once thought killed in action but who returns from war, you can begin to understand the level of celebration. Imagine the joy expressed by a parent having sent his or her one and only son or daughter off to war who had previously been notified of their loved one's death only to learn years later the same child was very much alive and well and returning home! What joy and celebration would take place!

The Son of God had, for thirty-three years, laid aside his divine attributes and became a man on a mission, a mission of redemption through self-sacrifice

(Phil. 2:6-8). The significance and existence of the entire universe succeeded or failed on those two hinges, the death and resurrection of the Son of God. No other two events in eternal history is as crucial. And when God's treasured son returned, "God exalted him to the highest place and gave him the name that is above every name, that at the name of Jesus every knee should bow in heaven and on earth, and every tongue acknowledge that Jesus is Lord, to the glory of God the Father" (Phil. 2:9-11).

Heaven's most precious treasure is now home and is seated at the right hand of the Father, talking to the Father every day about what He considers His greatest treasure: you and me! And He will continue doing so until we too are at home with Jesus.

Day 2:

EARTH'S GREATEST VICTORY WAS WON THERE

When Adam chose to join his wife, Eve, in the one thing God had told them not to do, everything changed. Not only did everything for the first couple change physically, emotionally, relationally, and spiritually, but the very Earth around them changed as well. Fruits and vegetables would no longer grow apart from "painful toil" (Gen. 3:19 NIV). Animals that once were sustained by a non-carnivorous diet ("everything that has the breath of life in it—I give every green plant for food" [Gen. 1:30 NIV]) were suddenly thrust into an environment known as the food chain where, for the most part, the smaller were consumed by the larger. The lamb that once lay down beside the lion now did so at its own peril. Roses, along with other plants and trees, began to grow thorns. Childbirth became agonizingly painful. The Garden of Eden was no more, worst of all, God no longer had pleasant walks and daily chats with His created humans.

Our limited, human minds cannot fully understand how different the world became the moment when

Adam and Eve chose to disregard the authority and honor of God, taking matters into their own hands, but we do know this: The Earth did, indeed, change. "The Fall of Man" brought about not only relational changes between God and His creation, but also between the created human beings.

How did the cross alter this sin-induced estrangement and upheaval? What does it mean that "Earth's greatest victory" was won at the cross?

The cross was the moment of the Earth's conception from its fallen state. One might call it the beginning of Earth's rebirth. What was to be its gestation period? Gestation periods vary depending on the species. It's 640 days for an elephant, 266 days for a human, and thirty-two days for a rabbit. What about Earth's gestation period? God alone knows, but at some point, the Earth will be restored to its former glory before "the Fall." Paul describes this in Romans 8:21-22: "The creation itself will be set free from its bondage to corruption and obtain the freedom of the glory of the children of God. For we know that the whole creation has been groaning together in the pains of childbirth until now." We are still in that "now" moment, uncertain of when the present pains of Earth's birthing, with all of its tragedies, conflicts, and sorrows will end and a "new heaven" (Rev. 2:1) will arrive.

What we can know for certain is this: Because of the cross, the "gestation period" has begun! The Father will send the Son back to the Earth to set in motion all that will make the world what it once was—when the lion will again lie down with the lamb, when conflicts will cease, and both personal and national wars will end (Isa. 11:6-9). And it all points back to the cross, when God, through Jesus, won the victory over death, hell, and the grave.

The Bible describes the moment of reclamation in Revelation chapter 5. The "Seven sealed scroll" seems to represent the "Title Deed" to the Earth and for a time John wept because it seemed no one was able to open it. Then John was told to "Weep no more; behold the Lion of the tribe of Judah, the Root of David, has conquered, so that he is able to open the scroll and its seven seals" (verse 5). Then John saw him, the lamb that had been slain, step up and take the book, initiating the reclamation of the Earth and everything associated with it.

Rejoice, O Earth, for at the cross your greatest victory was won!

Day 3:

OUR GREATEST ENEMY WAS DEFEATED THERE

It is widely understood that Satan is indeed the enemy of God, but what is also fully true is that he is also the enemy of man. He opposes the works of man in a myriad of ways, and despite his being banished from heaven along with tens of thousands of fallen angels that we refer to as demons, we are susceptible to his schemes. Without the ministry of the Holy Spirit within us, we are no match against him.

A question, though, begs to be asked: Having been cast from heaven and removed from power there, how is it that Satan still exists as the "power and prince of the air" and able to wreak havoc on Christians? The simple answer: The Bible speaks of heavens, and Satan was only banished from one!

The first time heaven is mentioned in the Bible is in Genesis 1:20. "Let the waters swarm with swarms of living creatures, and let birds fly above the earth across the expanse of heaven." Science has designated this heaven as the atmospheric heaven. This is the "first heaven" mentioned numerous times in scripture, and Satan still has power here.

In Genesis 15:5, God is having a conversation with Abram, explaining the future bounty of Abram's offspring: "Look toward the heaven, and number the stars if you are able to number them. Then he said to him, so shall your offspring be." This, of course, is in reference to the universe, which includes our galaxy and beyond. The Hubble Telescope is currently sending pictures back to us as it orbits the Earth in what is referred to here as the "second heaven," here too Satan still has power.

The third heaven is mentioned by Paul in 2 Corinthians 12:2 (NIV): "I know a man in Christ who fourteen years ago was caught up to the third heaven." This was describing his experience when God qualified him to be named among the apostles. He was brought into the third heaven to become an eyewitness to the risen Christ, a key qualification for apostleship. The Old Testament includes several mentions of the third heaven as God's dwelling place (Deut. 10:14; 1 Kings 8:30; Ps. 2:4).

A day is coming in the future when Satan and his followers will lose access to the first and second heavens and will be "hurled to the earth" (Rev. 12:13 NIV). Referenced in both the book of Daniel and Revelation, this will happen during a great war on Earth, commonly referred to as Armageddon, a war between Satan and God and their armies. It will end in the banishment of

Satan and his armies from both the heavens and the Earth. We're not there yet, but Satan's ultimate defeat is coming!

But when did Satan's defeat begin? It was at the cross. Genesis 3:13-15 NIV alludes to this ultimate battle and its conclusion when it makes this prophetic utterance: "He shall bruise your head and you shall bruise his heel." This was the conflict of the ages, and it was going to be settled once and for all at the cross. When Jesus bore our sin and shame on the cross, he took hold of death and carried it into the tomb, and when he came out of the grave the only things left behind were the grave clothes.

So today, take heart. The time is coming when Satan's power will be removed from the world forever because of the work of Jesus on the cross. At the cross, our greatest enemy has been defeated!

Day 4:

THE WINDOWS OF HOPE WERE RAISED THERE

Jesus came to Earth at a time in history where hope of reconciliation with God was hanging on by a mere thread. For the Israelites, God's chosen people, hope was fading in the silence. Four hundred years had passed since the last prophet proclaimed news, communication, warnings, anything from God. How do you hang on to hope of a future when your God has been silent for generations? And for the gentiles, those who at the time were living outside of the promises and protection of God, how could they possibly have any hope of connection or right standing with the Creator of the universe? Hope was either non-existent or fading fast—the setting of the arrival of Jesus into our world.

The same lack of hope is pervasive for our culture, thousands of years later, but in different ways. Occasionally our minds are ensnared with human reasoning—a common malady within all of us. It is never intentional; it just happens, perhaps even more so as technology allows us to venture more deeply into what was previously unknown. The Hubble Telescope, the marvel of technology that was launched in 1990, has travelled billions of miles as it orbits the Earth, and continues to send back images of wonders previously unseen and, in some cases, not even known to have existed prior to its deep gaze into space, exposing just how vast and wonderfully amazing the "second heaven" (universe) is. While the pictures sent back form the Hubble can cause us to marvel at the beauty and magnitude of the universe, when coupled with scientists telling us they're getting closer to finding what they call the "beginning" (referring to the "Big Bang" and answering the question of the "black hole" in space), those without a firm faith in scripture can be swayed and perplexed by these new but unsupported conclusions. "Scientific" discoveries by those with degrees and more knowledge than we have can often perplex those who have chosen the path of faith. Our minds can often be like that of a darting sparrow whose nest has been disturbed and, as a result, flies from tree to tree and from limb to limb searching for security in something familiar. Like the unsettledness of that sparrow, we too may occasionally lose our senses of security (our hope) when our faith nests have been disturbed and the confidences we once had in our futures become clouded, clouded to the point of questioning all that we once believed.

Where do we turn when our faith and hope have been shaken by the opinions of those who are considered the world's brightest minds? How does one come back from a place of doubt? How do we recover our faith and hope's erosion from personal tragedy or loss of relationship or any of the things that can choke off our sense of well-being and take us on a descending emotional journey?

It's back at the cross of Jesus where the windows of hope were thrust open by the tearing of the veil that separated all of us from God. Matthew 27 describes this moment of hope beautifully when the writer reveals that at the moment Jesus gave up his spirit, *"the curtain of the temple was torn in two from top to bottom."* The piece of fabric, eight to ten inches thick, separating not only most Israelites from God's presence but all of humanity as well, had been torn in two, symbolically and physically removing the barrier between God and His most precious creation (you and I and every other human who walks the Earth). That's hope! We have access to God through Jesus and his work on the cross. Despite loss. Despite doubt and confusion. Despite everything that is broken in this world, we can breathe the fresh air of hope because of what Jesus accomplished on the cross.

Day 5:

THE DOOR OF DELIVERANCE WAS OPENED THERE

Everyone at some time has found themselves in circumstances that seemed impossible to escape without suffering some kind of loss. The loss may be severe, even to the point of life change, or it may be only to the level of discomfort or embarrassment. But whatever the case, our instincts often drive us to find a way out that will result in the least amount of pain or consternation possible.

The Bible is replete with stories of men and women who were desperate to find their way out of unwanted and often unavoidable circumstances, sometimes of their own making (King David) and sometimes by God's assignment (Job). The well-known and often-told story of Jonah is a classic example of someone who, because of his resistance to God's plan, found himself inside a "great fish," a circumstance that, apart from God's help, had no doorway of escape (Jon. 1:17). When his circumstances became so dire he recognized that his *life was ebbing away* (Jon. 2:7), Jonah finally capitulated and almost immediately found himself free of the fish's belly and on dry ground.

For most of us, the escape from unwanted circumstances will not be quite as dramatic as Jonah's, but any kind of open door that provides an escape is a welcome relief.

The beauty of what God accomplished on the cross through the death of His son, Jesus, is that it opens the door of deliverance not only from day-to-day difficult circumstances, but also from the catastrophic end of the world predicted in Scripture. When the Apostle John wrote the book of Revelation, he was dictating the words of Jesus when he wrote, "Behold, I have set before you an open door, which no man is able to shut" (Rev. 3:8). What amazing words of encouragement expressed to the church at Philadelphia, located in what is now modern-day Turkey, a church known for its faithfulness to the Word of God and their Christian love for one another! This promise applies to believers in Christ today as well.

Much of what remains in the book of Revelation tells of a future that will be the most cataclysmic period ever experienced on Earth. For many, the reading of the book of Revelation is itself an experience that precipitates fear. The reality is this: Having to go through what is described in Revelation should strike fear in our hearts! Jesus himself said the conditions could not be compared to any other time in history (Matt. 24:21-22).

So should we live in daily fear of that time in the future? Should we live in fear and dread of the difficult circumstances we will experience in our lives (or are experiencing currently)? For anyone whose faith rests in Jesus Christ and what was accomplished through his death on the cross, subsequent burial, and ultimate resurrection, the answer is a resounding "NO!" Why? Because the door of deliverance was opened at the cross at a place known as "The Skull" on a hill called Golgotha.

When we put our faith in the death and resurrection of Jesus, the fear of death loses its sting and the grave suffers defeat (1 Cor. 15:55 KJV). That faith in the work of Jesus on the cross is the "open door" through which our deliverance from Earth's future catastrophe will come.

The door of deliverance was opened at the cross, not only from the future judgement of the world but also from the dread of personal judgment regarding our sins. The cross is not always an escape from the struggles of this life, but it provides the internal satisfaction that what we're going through is essential to understanding the ultimate deliverance offered by the cross. All the wrongs we have thought upon or acted out will no longer enter the mind of the Heavenly Father because of what the Son did on the cross. "For I will be merciful to their unrighteousness, and their sins and iniquities will I remember no more" (Heb. 8:11).

Through the Cross we have been placed into the hands of one who has chosen to deliver us from all the wrongs we have ever done.

Day 6:

OCEANS OF GRACE
WERE EXPOSED THERE

When John Newton, a onetime slave trader, penned the words "Amazing grace, how sweet the sound," he could not have known that his song, "Amazing Grace," which he wrote in 1772, would be the hymn most often sung ever since. It seems as though God wanted to use the hymn to expose the world to the extensiveness of the grace made available to all of humanity through the death of Jesus on the cross. Newton, who spent much of his young life on the sea, would have routinely viewed the immensity of the ocean with its perils and would certainly have understood the comparison of the breadth of the ocean with the immeasurable expanse of God's grace.

However, it is easy to miss the importance of the vastness of God's grace and our need for it in our lives. It's something we have in common with the first-century Jews who, in many ways, misinterpreted Jesus and his mission on earth.

The week leading up to the crucifixion started with great enthusiasm—the miracle worker's fame was expanding rapidly as throngs of people began to see with their own eyes what they had previously only heard about. The stories coming out of Galilee of healings, resurrections of the dead, and feeding of thousands from a little boy's lunch were no longer just rumors. Hundreds were now seeing blind eyes opened, men who were once lame now running, and those with once incurable diseases being made well again. What great celebrations must have taken place throughout the city of Jerusalem as reports of one healing after another began to swirl, suggesting that the "Promised One" had come. Their shouts of "Hosanna the Son of David" were clearly identifying Jesus as the Messiah. They were all aware of the covenant God had made with King David (2 Sam. 7; 1 Chron. 17:11-14; 2 Chron. 6:16) that told of a future day when a king out of the lineage of David would come and bring peace to the Earth. There was a general assumption amongst the Jewish people that the day was about to arrive in the person of Jesus and that he soon would, as Messiah, begin his reign on earth, freeing them from the oppression of Roman rule.

God's plan, however, was decidedly different, for Jesus had a much bigger kingdom in mind than what lived in the minds of those looking for a Jewish Messiah. Jesus was on a mission that was incomprehensible even to those closest to him; a mission that would settle man's sin question forever and expand God's grace to all people. A new kind of sacrifice was coming that would once and for all pay for the sins of humanity past, present, and future. This was a radical change, an ocean of grace that up to this point was unavailable through the sacrificial lambs that were offered by and for the Jewish people. For centuries, sacrifices had been made for God's chosen people that served merely as a bulldozer that kept piling up and pushing aside the sins of the people to ultimately be dealt with at another time. You don't deal with that kind of muck with a mere garden hose. It would take an ocean of grace to cover the sins of not just the Jews but the gentiles and all of humanity going forward.

This sacrifice, unlike the sacrifice of an animal that only transferred sin to the next Passover, would completely remove sin from the hearts of believers. As John the Baptist had proclaimed, "Look, the Lamb of God, who takes away the sins of the world!" (John 1:29 NIV). There was never a lamb like this Lamb who did not merely transfer sin but took all sin onto himself. That is grace! That is unmerited favor! Once a person, whether Jew or Gentile, accepted the reality of that sacrifice on his or her behalf, their sin would be forgiven, and their wickedness remembered no more (Heb. 8:12 NIV).

The cross became the release point from which oceans of grace were exposed. The blood of Jesus Christ is limitless in its power to cleanse. Regardless of how many come placing their faith in Him, an ocean of grace awaits them.

Day 7:

THE GREATEST KINDNESS WAS SHOWN THERE

Roddy Reid was an upperclassman that every young freshman could look up too. He was a tall athletic type without the arrogance that is often associated with those who have superior athletic skills. He even made underclassmen like me feel important. His younger years had been spent in South America where his parents where missionaries. Once he reached high school, there was no place for him to continue his education and as a result Roddy came to live with his aunt and uncle in the little town of Jay, Oklahoma. We not only attended the same school; we also attended the same church. Though I was three years his junior, he never made me feel like anything but an equal. Roddy, who was the best Christian teenager I had ever known, had significant influence in my life.

He went on to play college basketball while I finished high school and entered the military service, and we mostly lost contact. Except for knowing he married his high school sweetheart and moved to the state of Washington, I knew little of Roddy's life until one day a friend contacted me and wanted to know if I had heard about how Roddy had drowned trying to save the lives of two younger boys (not his own) in the cold waters off the coast of Washington while on a fishing trip. Because of rough seas, both boys had fallen into the water. Roddy instinctively jumped in to save them, only to be overcome by the rough seas and cold water as he was getting them safely back into the boat. Though it had been nearly fifteen years since I had seen him, this was the Roddy Reid I had known. Kindness to his friends even at the peril of his own life.

As much kindness as it took for Roddy to sacrifice his life in an effort to save his young friends, how much more kindness does it take for someone to sacrifice his or her life for someone who most would consider to be someone who doesn't deserve it? We can never understand kindness in its fullest sense until we understand the immense difference between the holiness of God and the unholy nature of man. This is especially true in our Western culture, in which we have a sense that God comes alongside us in our self-elevated thoughts of our own worthiness and we enlist religious practices to make ourselves look better. We have an elevated sense of our own goodness, which clouds our ability to see how perfect God is, keeping us from recognizing how foolish (in human terms) it was for Jesus to die on our behalves.

But he did. He moved toward us first. The writer of the book of Romans says it best when he wrote, "You see, at just the right time, when we were still powerless, Christ died for the ungodly. Very rarely will anyone die for a righteous person, though for a good person someone might possibly dare to die. But God demonstrates his own love for us in this: While we were still sinners, Christ died for us" (Rom. 5:6-8 NIV). Before a person establishes his or her faith in Jesus, God the Father, despite how far down the scale of importance He is to us, begins to set up all types of connecting points that may stimulate a deepening interest in Him. That deepening interest will ultimately attract a seeking heart to the Word of God, the Bible, which is vital because it is the Bible that provides the impetus for someone's hunger to know God. Quoting Jesus, John wrote, "Very truly I tell you, whoever hears my word and believes in him who sent me has eternal life and will not be judged but has crossed over from death to life" (John 5:24 NIV). On another occasion Jesus said, "No one can come to me unless the Father who sent me draws them" (John 5:24 NIV).

What amazing kindness is shown to us! When we had little or no interest in Him and very little knowledge of Him, He loved us so much that He provided His only Son to receive and experience judgment for our sins (1 Pet. 2:24 NIV). We were so spiritually insensitive that the Apostle Paul referred to our condition as dead, so spiritually insensitive that we did not have the capacity for a relationship with Him. The cross began to awaken us to the reality that He actually wanted a relationship with us, even with those who had spent such a long time avoiding such a relationship.

Soak in this remarkable statement about God and His incredible kindness to us: "But because of his great love for us, God, who is rich in mercy, made us alive with Christ even when we were dread in transgressions—it is by grace you have been saved. And God raised us up with Christ and seated us with him in heavenly realms in Jesus Christ, in order that in the coming ages he might show us the incomparable riches of his grace, expressed in his kindness to us in Christ Jesus. For by grace are you saved, through faith—and that not of yourselves, it is the gift of God—not by works, so that no one can boast" (Eph. 2:4-9).

The greatest kindness exploded upon all mankind as Jesus hung on the cross and willingly accepted the penalty that must be paid for sin.

Day 8:

RIVERS OF MERCY WERE RELEASED THERE

J ust how abundant are the mercies of God the Father? From our human, earthly perspective they, of course, cannot be fully measured, but what we do know is that it is at the cross they were expressively released. Ever since the fall of man in the Garden of Eden, the justice and judgment of God have been waiting to render the inevitable ruling that his holiness demanded. The courts of heaven had determined that the penalty of sin was death—not just human death, the kind that separates a human being from his or her existence on Earth. No, this death was to be much more substantial than physical death; this death meant separation from the Creator Himself and all the attributes associated with Him. Our limited, human imaginations are not capable of fathoming the great loss associated with a disconnection from the Divine!

One of these losses, though, is the ever-present expression of mercy: "Because of the Lord's great love we are not consumed for his compassions (mercies) never fail. They are new every morning; great is your faithfulness" (Lam. 3:22-23). Much can be said about God's mercies, especially when you consider how desperate our lives are with their many imperfections—we find our need of large doses of God's mercy every day. If grace can be described as "getting something we do not deserve," then mercy can be described as "not getting something we do deserve." If not for God's great mercy, no one would ever reach the place of experiencing the grace of God that comes through faith. It is by God's mercy that keeps us from experiencing the wages of sin, giving us more time to experience the saving grace of God.

On the cross, Jesus called upon the Father to "forgive them for they know not what they do" (Luke 23:24). He was expressly speaking on behalf of the throngs of people, mostly Jewish, who had hailed him as Messiah one day and then cried out to have him crucified the next. Jesus's request, asking the Father to forgive them, was without question a plea on behalf of thousands of people for God's mercy. He was giving them more time.

Did the Father answer that prayer? Indeed He did. The answer came fifty days after the resurrection of Jesus. After grain harvest there was a celebration among the Jews referred to as the Feast of First Fruits. This special day was also known as "The Day of Pentecost." It was a seasonal celebration among Jewish people everywhere but especially in Jerusalem, where Jewish families would gather, traveling many miles to be a part of the Passover celebration.

Thousands had gathered in Jerusalem when the Heavenly Father began to not only answer His son's prayers of forgiveness and mercy, but also Jesus's promise to his apostles about the coming of the Holy Spirit. When the Spirit came, it was in great power that gave the apostles the miraculous ability to speak in languages they had never heard before. This was an amazing and miraculous accommodation for the many who had come from "every nation under heaven" (Acts 2:5 NIV). What thousands were about to hear was a message of salvation in their own language spoken by uneducated men from Galilee.

In the crowd were most likely some of the same who, seven weeks earlier had cried "Crucify him," the same people who were urging Pilate to scourge Jesus with a whip and let his blood be on their hands. Today, on this day of Pentecost, they were hearing Jesus's followers tell a story of one who had come to offer forgiveness for sin, with the opportunity to be forever cleansed by the blood of his sacrifice and experience a resurrection that Jesus himself had demonstrated. That day three thousand souls came to seek forgiveness, and that was just the beginning. For more than two-thousand years since, millions of others have placed their faith in the forgiveness offered by Jesus.

And it all started at the cross, where rivers of mercy were released, and the tributaries of mercy are continuing to flow by the blood of Jesus into "every nation under heaven" (Acts 2:5 NIV).

Day 9:

FOUNTAINS OF CLEANSING BURST FORTH THERE

In October of 2018 Florence, a rain-laden hurricane, slowly moved across the Carolinas, depositing so much water that creeks, rivers, lakes and ponds could not contain the more than thirty inches of rain that fell over three-day period. Land and property not listed as being in flood zones and had never flooded before became inundated with flood waters from the Cape Fear River and its tributaries. Days later when the waters finally receded, what was left were thousands of homes caked with mud, muck and mold, with more damage than could have been imagined. The initial clean up took months, and the rebuilding will continue for many years to come. It took a herculean effort by thousands of volunteers and contractors to purge these homes from the filth left behind. For weeks after the storm, workers told stories day after day of the filth left on their bodies after spending days in crawl spaces beneath the homes, pumping out water, tearing out moldy sheetrock and sewage-soaked insulation. The relief experienced during the evening baths and showers following those days of hard labor was often described as "nothing short of heaven."

For every day spent in and under the flooded houses, the evening shower was a necessary part of the worker's daily ritual. As cleansing and refreshing as those evening showers may have been for the workers, they only had the capacity to clean their bodies. There is, however, a cleansing that goes deeper and provides a far greater sense of satisfaction, and it never has to be repeated. It is the cleansing power of the blood of Jesus that was shed on the cross on Golgotha's hill.

The poet William Cowper (1731-1800) suffered from bouts of depression for many years, and it was during one of these anguished bouts that he attempted suicide and was assigned a period of time to a private asylum. Even during his emotional struggles, however, he became one of England's most beloved poets and songwriters. In the first stanza of his song "There Is a Fountain Filled with Blood," Cowper wrote that this fountain is "Drawn from Immanuel's veins; And sinners plunged beneath that flood lose all their guilty stains." When we begin to understand how deeply the stain of sin has gone into every human being, we understand how the miracle of the cleansing power of Jesus's blood falls into the "wonder of wonders" category.

And this cleansing goes far beyond the surface. Not only is the cleansing deep, but it is also thorough. In Psalm 51:7 (KJV), the psalmist writes, "Wash me, and I shall be whiter than snow." A believer in Jesus is so thoroughly cleansed by the blood of Christ that when the sin-searching "cherubim" (Gen. 3:24) wields the "flaming sword" able to expose every human flaw, no evidence of sin can be found to have existed in the redeemed.

Read how this cleansing is described by the apostle Paul: "Therefore, if anyone is in Christ, the new creation has come: The old has gone, the new is here!" (2 Cor. 5:17 NIV). And "God made him who knew no sin to be sin for us, so that in him we might become the righteousness of God" (2 Cor. 5:21 NIV).

It is the blood from the bruised and broken body of Jesus that cleanses with such completeness. Jesus considered it so significant that he instituted what has come to be known as communion, a time when a believer steps back to reflect on how he or she is living life and to call into remembrance the price Jesus paid for the sin that was not his own. What an amazing exchange took place. The apostle Peter continues this theme when he wrote "the righteous for the unrighteous" (I Peter 1:18 NIV).

The fountain of cleansing did indeed burst forth from the cross.

Day 10:

MOUNTAINS OF OPPORTUNITY BEGAN THERE

Considering Jesus's numerous and significant works, his words to the disciples, "whoever believes in me will do the works I have been doing, and will do even greater things than these" (John 14:12 NIV) must have seemed to them as though he was speaking metaphorically. How could this possibly be? They had watched Jesus heal the sick, open blind eyes, cause deaf people to hear and the dumb to speak, and had even seen him raise the dead back to life! It would have seemed preposterous for uneducated fishermen to do something even close to the magnitude of what Jesus had done, much less to do even greater things!

That is until they saw him die like no other man and come back to life as only God could do. Some had followed but "far off," and others were plagued with doubting. Peter denied him on that fateful night when Jesus was led off by Roman soldiers, and "all" had become gripped with fear and forsaken him. This is the "greater works" crowd that Jesus was talking about. How did these "greater works" become reality?

The only possible explanation is the cross, followed by and culminating in the resurrection. We can only begin to imagine what may have gone on in the disciples' minds when they began to witness Jesus's teaching become true in the reality of their personal experiences connected to the cross. They now understood that the bread Jesus broke at the "Last Supper" was, in fact, a picture of his own body being broken. Isaiah's writing had come to light in the darkness of the cross: "He was pierced for our transgression, he was crushed for our iniquities" (Isa. 53:5). These words were no longer writings on pages they had studied and memorized as children; they became a reality they had witnessed and experienced.

That first Easter allowed the followers of Jesus to believe on a whole new level. Fear had been replaced by faith. Doubting had turned into determination. Denial had been transformed into dedication. And as for "far off" following? Well, it had become a thing of the past; the disciples became known as men who "had been with Jesus" (Acts 4:13 NIV).

Because of the cross and the resurrection that followed, a whole new world lay before them. Most of these early followers were Galileans who had never traveled beyond that region; they had now been commissioned to "go and make disciples of all nations" (Matt. 28:19 NIV). What a mountainous expansion of opportunity! And as they obeyed this call, they saw many mighty works of God. Language barriers were miraculously removed, chains once tightly locked fell off, and even prison doors seemed to open on their own. These things had never happened before, and these experiences continued not only to enlarge their understanding of just how great this God was who they were serving, but also to solidify their unquestioned belief in Jesus as the "promised one."

Opportunities are unique in that although they have been offered, you cannot experience the pleasure of the realization or reality of the opportunity until you take some action. In the secular world it's referred to as "taking advantage of the opportunity," In the Christian world, the action is called "faith." In either case, the materialization of the opportunity demands action of some kind. While the Bible doesn't include all of the experiences of the disciples nor those of the other followers of Jesus, what it does tell us is that they responded in faith to opportunities set before them, for millions around the world have become followers of Jesus because of it.

You may be one of them. If you are, it is because you have found your way to the cross and now have a mountain range of opportunities waiting for you as well.

Day 11:

OUR STRENGTH IS RENEWED THERE

Renewal is necessary in several different ways (physically, emotionally, creatively) at many points throughout a person's life. By far the greatest need for renewal we have is when our spiritual strength seems to have ebbed away. Why is it that we lose our spiritual strength, and when we do, how can it be renewed?

Numbers 21, in the Old Testament, captures a time when God's people had become dissatisfied with the provision God was giving them and the leadership He was providing. Their rebellious complaining became so great that it was keeping them from making any progress toward their ultimate homeland destination. That lack of movement alone should have been an indication that something was missing, that something was "off," but instead of pausing to examine their hearts and expressing gratitude to God for His provision and leadership, they simply continued to grumble and complain.

Eventually God determined His people were not going to figure it out on their own and that the only remedy for their rebellion was to send a plague of fiery serpents. As people began to die from the serpents' poisonous bites, the Israelites began to cry out to Moses, their leader, cries of fear and confession for their rebellion against both Moses and God began to quickly replace their complaints.

Like the Israelites, our spiritual strength becomes depleted when we lose confidence in who God is. When our circumstances don't line up with our expectations from life or from God, it's easy to become confused and wonder if God really is who He says He is—to lose our strength spiritually and to drift slowly away from the one relationship that is our source of both life and strength, and it is at the cross that we receive life and renewal of our spiritual strength. The cross is the source of renewal, both for the Israelites in the desert and for us 3500 years later!

You see, hearing the complaints of his followers, Moses prayed to God on their behalf and was instructed to mold a bronze serpent and place it upon a pole so it could be seen throughout the camp. All the people had to do was to "look" at the bronze serpent to be healed physically and, through their faith and confidence in God's promise, to be renewed and healed spiritually as well. What does this have to do with the cross? Everything! Paul wrote in Galatians 3:13 (NIV), "Christ redeemed us from the curse of the law by becoming a curse for us, for it is written: Cursed is everyone who is hung on a pole." The curse goes all the way back to that moment in the Garden of Eden when Adam and

Eve succumbed to the temptation of Satan. From that moment on, they and all of humanity would be under the curse of sin, and sin's punishment is death. The "wages of sin is death" (Rom. 6:23 NIV), and the only remedy for our sins, both for the Israelites and for us now is to draw near to God, through faith, and what He did on the cross.

The bronze serpent is a "type" of Christ, a representation of Jesus hanging on the cross nearly 1500 years later when he took the curse of sin upon himself and "became a curse for us." Jesus himself even refers to the story when he was talking to Nicodemus, a high-ranking teacher among the Jews, saying, "Just as Moses lifted up the snake in the wilderness so the son of man must be lifted up, that everyone who believes may have eternal life in him" (John 3:14-15). The faith that it took for the Israelites who had been bitten to look to the bronze serpent for renewal of their strength (both physically and spiritually) is the same faith that is required of us today.

Up until our moment of faith in Jesus's work on the cross, we are relegated to live our lives on the strength of human determination. Our religious efforts without divine enablement are described by Charles Spurgeon, an eighteenth-century preacher, in this way: "The river of God is full of water; but not one drop of it flows from earthly springs."

The headwaters of strength that will carry us into the next life begin at the cross.

Day 12:

THE GREATEST OF FRIENDSHIPS WAS INITIATED THERE

How does one describe friendship? Everyone will have their own unique twist to what friendship means to them, but one of the common denominators is "friends get along." That is how I would describe the friendship that existed between God and Earth's first couple, Adam and Eve—they got along. They got along so well, in fact, that God spoke with them about some simple rules of garden living, and for a time (we don't know how long) they were able to enjoy the indescribable beauty of Eden and apparent friendship with God.

It is hard to comprehend all that was lost when Adam and Eve ate of the forbidden fruit from the tree of the knowledge of good and evil. One thing we do know is that a new emotion, fear, had crowded out the sense of peace and contentment within them. Trust, an essential feature of a true friendship, had now been eroded as well

Let's fast-forward to the day Jesus died on the cross and meet two men, both criminals, who had lived their lives estranged from God, one on the right and one on the left. They had joined the scribes and elders in mocking Jesus who were saying, "He saved others; he cannot save himself. He is the king of Israel; Let him come down now from the cross, and we will believe in him. He trusts in God; let God deliver him now, if he desires him. For he said "I am the son of God"". And the robbers who were crucified with him also reviled him in the same way" (Matt. 27-44ESV).

One of those hanging there with him was in time smitten with conviction as he observed the manner in which Jesus was dying. When Jesus asked the Father to forgive his tormentors, even this hardened criminal was moved to admit that there was something decidedly different about this man Jesus. In fact, he offered this retort to the other thief: "Do you not fear God, since you are under the same sentence of condemnation? And we indeed justly, for we are receiving the due reward of our deeds; but this man has done nothing wrong." In the same breath, the criminal makes one last appeal, "Jesus, remember me when you come into your kingdom" (Luke 23:40-43ESV).

Within those few hours, not only was an amazing friendship established, but an eternal relationship was established as well. Jesus responded, "Truly, I say to you, today you will be with me in Paradise" (Luke 23:43 ESV). Jesus had heard the cry of a broken heart and, as a result, was not going to allow him to hang there without hope. Nothing more is ever said about the thieves that were crucified with Jesus that day.

Apparently the most important thing that can be said about this thief's life was what Jesus said to him: "you will be with me."

There is no greater picture of Jesus being a friend to sinners than this story. Earlier in Matthew 11:19 Jesus had been described as one who was a friend to sinners. As unbelievable as it may seem, here he was telling this unworthy man, who a few hours earlier was ridiculing Jesus, and now Jesus is telling him He wanted to spend the rest of the day with him. So just as soon as Jesus was finished with dying, there they were spending time together as friends.

It was at the Cross that Jesus not only proved his love, but he also demonstrated his friendship. "Greater love has no man than this, that someone lay down his life for his friends" (John 15:13 ESV).

Day 13:

THE APEX OF FORGIVENESS WAS REACHED THERE

When Jesus was responding to the disciple's request, "Lord teach us to pray," he replied by giving them what is commonly known as "The Lord's Prayer." A more accurate description would be "The Lord's Sample Prayer," for in this simple prayer Jesus includes the line, "Forgive us our sins." As a result of living a life of perfection, Jesus had no sins that needed forgiving. This perfect Savior was teaching an imperfect humanity how much we need to recognize our own shortcomings by asking for forgiveness.

The cross where Jesus gave his life is the setting where God chose to display the ultimate demonstration of divine forgiveness. This kind of forgiveness cannot be captured or computed by the human mind without the supernatural enablement of the Holy Spirit. To help us understand, the Holy Spirit leads us down the path of faith, for God knows faith is the only thing that will allow us to access sacred regions where divine forgiveness dwells. Having once entered this understanding of forgiveness, we learn it is not for a mere visit. The status of "forgiven" becomes an eternal dwelling place. One of the privileges of being completely forgiven is being able to spend time with God and feel comfortable doing it.

That level of comfort we discover when we are forgiven is the same level Jesus experiences with his Father. We can now join Jesus and respond to God the Father in the most intimate of terms, Abba Father. Abba Father is first mentioned in the Bible when Jesus was agonizing in a garden known as Gethsemane, where he prayed, "Abba Father." He said, "Everything is possible for you. Take this cup from me. Yet not what I will, but what you will" (Mark 14:36 NIV). This was the eve of the crucifixion, and in this moment we are given a window into the intimacy that exists between God the Father and God the Son. It is difficult to miss the loving sacredness in the words "Abba Father" as both the Father and the Son knew what the next few hours held for them both.

Later, through the Apostle Paul's letter to the Galatians, we learn that because of Jesus's sacrifice on the cross, God could extend to all such complete forgiveness that the most undeserving could join him in calling upon God as Abba Father by simply placing their faith in Jesus Christ and accepting the forgiveness offered through his death. "Because you are his sons, God sent the Spirit of his Son into our hearts, the Spirit who calls out, Abba, Father" (Gal. 4:6 NIV).

The forgiveness extended at the cross is so extensive that it removes all of the barriers between totally sinful man and a completely holy God. Nothing else can possibly explain how this writer and all who read this are given the privilege of calling God "Daddy," the Aramaic translation of "Abba Father." The intercessory prayer Jesus prayed over Jerusalem while hanging on the cross, "Father forgive them for the know not what they do," extends to every person in every city, town, and village to this very day.

God's forgiveness, just like his grace and mercy, has no boundary. It extends into the farthest reaches of the Earth and into the darkest reaches of the human heart. Nothing is beyond the length of the Father's loving arms.

Day 14:

MAN'S PEACE WITH GOD WAS ESTABLISHED THERE

U nless it has been educated out of a person's inmost thoughts, the sense of God's existence and humanity's being at odds with Him dwells within the bosom of every person (Rom. 1:18-23). Sin has left an indelible mark upon every soul, and before a person's conscience has become completely seared, he has a sense of dread, even condemnation, regarding those sins. The cross of Christ is the only suitable escape, not just from the dread of condemnation but from the condemnation itself.

But not everyone sees the cross as the way of escape. Many have tried to avoid the cross, and others have tried to avoid God altogether. Some sought to create a different god, one more suitable to their lifestyles, while others have adopted agnosticism as the basis for their belief system. Some have even fled to the assumed "refuge" of atheism. While all of these approaches seem to provide some degree of satisfaction and peace, they are ultimately limited, for those who have chosen anything other than God and His word as a refuge find the footing unreliable, especially in crisis. Even the French philosopher Voltaire, known for his "enlightenment" writings and his use of wit in criticizing Christianity, said as he was dying, "For all the money in Europe I would not want to see another unbeliever die." His atheism had robbed him of his wit and humor in his last hours, and he died a fearful man, lacking peace.

As important as peace with God is as a person approaches life's final moments, peace with God is not just for one's dying hour, for peace *with* God is the great enabler of the "peace *of* God," which is life's companion that enables us to live life with joyous fulfillment. That same peace provides a sure confidence of the future. Being rich or poor or healthy or ill has little to do with joyous fulfillment; internal peace and satisfaction are commodities that come only when a person places their faith in the finished work of the cross.

Nothing is more celebrated than a country's military returning victorious from war. The embattled soldiers return home where they enjoy a rest that has been assured by the peace that was won on the battlefield. Concerning the Cross, the battle was for the souls of mankind and no ordinary soldier could have fought that battle. On that battlefield, only someone with divine qualifications could, with eternal intent, die an undeserved death for the sake of a hell-deserving humanity. Peace, won at the cross for all who believe, resulted in the ever-abiding comfort of the Holy Spirit, from which comes the "peace of God."

The promise of peace came from the lips of Jesus himself. "These things I have spoken to you while I am still with you. But the Helper, the Holy Spirit, whom the Father will send in my name, he will teach you all things and bring to your remembrance all that I have said to you. Peace I leave with you; my peace I give to you. Not as the world gives do I give to you. Let not your hearts be troubled, neither let them be afraid" (John 14:25-27 ESV).

The cross is the distribution point of peace, for all of time and eternity.

Day 15:

ALL OF GOD'S BENEFITS WERE DISTRIBUTED THERE

When the Savior gave his life on the cross, he opened the door to all, not only to be *called* the "children of God" but to actually *be* the children of God. The concept of humans as joint heirs with Jesus is another of the remarkable features that come to us when we place our faith in Jesus, and it's described in scripture in two ways: birth and adoption. Jesus told Nicodemus, a well-educated religious leader, that he "must be born again" (John 3:7). The apostle Paul wrote, in Galatians 4:5, that Jesus came "so that we might receive the adoption as sons." So which is it? Are we born or adopted into God's family? The answer is both.

When someone is "born again," it is the work of the Holy Spirit in partnership with the Word of God to bring them to the point of faith until that faith crosses the threshold of belief. In an instant, the Spirit of God becomes embodied into their soul and a new birth springs forth—they become a child of God through the experience of being "born again." "For you have been born again, not of perishable seed, but of imperishable, through the living and enduring word of God" (1 Pet. 1:23 NIV). As this new journey begins along with ever-expanding new insights, the elaborateness of the benefits of this new birth begin an unfolding drama with lifelong duration.

A parallel event in the unfolding drama of rebirth is the adoption of the believer into the family of God. The term "adoption" in the Bible as it relates to Jewish society is related more to the practice of the Jewish Bar Mitzvah than it is to our common understanding of adoption today. In the traditional Jewish family, when a boy reaches the age of thirteen, he is given the prerogative to go through the Bar Mitzvah and given full adult privileges and responsibilities, including the rights to his father's inheritance.

In the same way, when a person becomes a Christian by virtue of the new birth, they also receive the adoption (Bar Mitzvah) with all the rights to the Father's fortune. When we put our faith in Jesus Christ, we become joint heirs with him as well!

What happens when one has experienced these parallel events, the new birth which places us into the family of God, and the adoption, which gives us all the benefits of being a member of the family of God? Certainly, all of the benefits already mentioned in previous devotions: hope, deliverance, grace, kindness, opportunity, strength, friendship, forgiveness, and peace, as well as those in the pages that follow, such as joy, redemption, love, and righteousness. On top of these, we can add that we are able to share in God's pleasures and riches. We also gain a sense of belonging to a family. We become brothers of Christ, in a sense, and siblings of all of those who have put their faith in Jesus. We now have the ability to grow into full maturity in Christ. Presently, we don't know and cannot comprehend the fullness of being adopted and having full adult privileges and probably will not know on this side of eternity. This is such an amazing truth that it is difficult to fit into the human brain. However wonderful the things the Holy Spirit has unveiled to us concerning the realities of God, there is more to come. "But as it is written, eye hath not seen, nor ear heard, neither have entered into the heart of man, the things which God hath prepared for them that love him" (1 Cor. 2:9 KJV).

All of this and more happened over two thousand years ago at eternity's distribution station at a place then known as Golgotha, the place of the skull, a place known today as Mt. Calvary, the place of the cross where all of God's benefits were distributed.

Day 16:

THE FOUNDATION STONE OF JOY WAS LAID THERE

These words of Jesus, "I have come that they may have life, and have it to the full" (John 10:10) would not have been possible without Calvary's cross, where his kingship had been mocked with a crown of thorns. Little did the Roman soldiers know they had, in effect, crowned him as the king of love. King David wrote in Psalm 16:11 how the "path of life" was the result of the path of death Jesus endured on the cross. Believers now understand that Jesus's suffering and death were essential in providing eternal life for all who would place their faith in him. Later in the same verse, David expressed we would have "eternal pleasures" at the right hand of the Savior.

In John 10:10, Jesus tells us that believers do not need to wait until a future in heaven to experience the joy of salvation. When the Apostle Paul was writing to the Christians in Rome, at a time when the Roman believers were experiencing bitter persecution, he wrote these encouraging words: "May the God of hope fill you with all joy and peace as you trust in him, so that you may overflow with hope by the power of the Holy Spirit" (Rom. 15:13 NIV). The joy they could experience through the cross would come from within them despite their circumstances, and its touch-point was the cross. The Apostle Peter was convinced that joy authenticates a person's faith, writing that "...the authenticity of your faith—more precious than gold, which perishes even though refined by fire—may result in praise, glory, and honor at the revelation of Jesus Christ. Though you have not seen him, you love him, and though you do not see him now, you believe in him and rejoice with inexpressible and glorious joy" (1 Pet. 1:7-8 NIV). That kind of joy was first announced to the shepherds watching over their sheep in the grass-laden hills surrounding Bethlehem. In that bright, star-filled, cold night came the angelic announcement, "Fear not, for behold, I bring you good news of great joy that will be to all people. For unto you is born this day in the city of David a Savior, who is Christ the Lord" (Luke 2:10-11 NIV).

The phrase in the angelic announcement that "a Savior is born" reveals the connecting point between Jesus at his birth and Jesus at his cross, making the lyrics "the baby you deliver will soon deliver you" in Mark Lowry's song "Mary Did You Know," so powerfully poignant. And that deliverance took place at Calvary. The idea of a suffering Savior was not a new thought, for in the book of Isaiah we read, "Surely he took our pain and bore our suffering, yet we considered him punished by God, stricken by him, and afflicted. But he was pierced for our transgression, he was crushed for our iniquities; the punishment that brought us peace was on him, and by his wounds we are healed" (Isa. 53:4-5 NIV).

The peace Jesus provided on the cross was the foundation stone for the joy that is now afforded to every person whose faith rests in the Savior.

Day 17:

ALL OUR INIQUITIES WERE NAILED THERE

The point of Jesus's substitutionary death on the cross becomes more powerfully impactful to us as our comprehension of the sinful nature of man enlarges. It's often true that when someone begins the Christian life at a young age, it takes them a few years to come to the realization of just how dreadful the human nature is, which is possibly the reason why the cross becomes more and more dear to us as we mature. As we grow older and the Bible peels away our self-deception and we discover just how incorrigibly desperate we are without God, we become increasingly more grateful for Jesus's sacrificial death in our place. It is not just a matter of what we have done or what we have said that exposes our sin natures, for even our thoughts and ideas are on record with God—"The Lord knows all human plans; he knows they are futile" (Ps 94:11 NIV).

The final analysis of the human heart is recorded by the Old Testament prophet, Jeremiah: "The heart is deceitful above all things, and is desperately wicked: who can know it?" (Jer. 17:9 KJV). He goes on to describe the desperate conditions of the human heart when he writes, "Can an Ethiopian change his skin or a leopard its spots? Neither can you do good who are accustomed to doing evil" (Jer. 13:23 NIV). For most of us, it is difficult to accept that our natural instinct is bent toward evil. But the reality is this: Even good actions, if we probe deeply enough, often expose self-serving motives. "Evil customs" are as impossible to change as Ethiopian skin or leopard spots. The Creator himself just brings about the conditions that would allow for such a miracle.

To deal with "evil customs" was the aim of the miracle that occurred in the city of Nazareth where a virgin whose name was Mary was visited by the angel Gabriel. He revealed to her the plan that included her miraculously conceiving and bearing a child who she was to name Jesus. This Jesus was to be the "evil customs" breaker. Amazingly, the act of someone placing their faith in Jesus Christ not only breaks the custom of evil but also provides a whole new way of looking at life by giving a new heart and mind. That promise was first made to Israel through the prophet Ezekiel: "I will give you a new heart and put a new spirt within you" (Ezek. 36:26 NIV).

A person's faith in Jesus identifies them with the crucified Christ: "I have been crucified with Christ and I no longer live, but Christ lives in me. The life I now live in the body I live by faith in the Son of God, who loved me and gave himself for me" (Gal. 2:20 NIV).

What happened to the iniquity customs of an old heart? They were nailed to the cross: "When you were dead in your sin and in the uncircumcision of your flesh, God made you alive with Christ. He forgave all our sins, having canceled the charge of our legal indebtedness, which stood against us and condemned us; he has taken it away, nailing it to the cross" (Col. 2:13-14 NIV).

There are no plans for Jesus to return to the cross; therefore, all past, present, and future iniquities were nailed there.

Day 18:

OUR REDEMPTION
WAS PURCHASED THERE

S *aving Private Ryan* is an epic World War II cinematic journey that, since its release in 1998, has taken its viewers along with a small group of Army rangers on the harrowing mission of rescuing an American paratrooper from behind enemy lines. The film is filled with gripping scenes of the brutality of war and displays the bravery and sacrifice of the men on the mission to find Private Ryan and return him to his family. Although successful in their mission, it was not without severe cost, and at the end of his life, Ryan asks his wife, while standing at the grave of one of his rescuers, if he is a good man, worthy of the sacrifice. She tells him he is.

Although not historically accurate, the movie is a vivid portrayal of the concept of redemption and its cost, and from beginning to end the Bible is the story of God seeking to get his most prized possession, mankind, back. It is the story of how this once-honored creature God called man had the perfection of everything, including unbroken friendship with God that included daily walks with him through the most enchanting garden ever created, fell from grace into sin. Inferiority, insecurity, inadequacy, and guilt were not originally found in Adam and Eve's emotional makeup. Their relationships were of perfect harmony. Food was at their fingertips, and the work required to produce it did not so much as activate the sweat glands. It was the best of worlds.

So what happened? It's what happens to everyone— curiosity and the desire to want something forbidden become the drivers of decision-making. Couple that with false but enticing words from Satan, and together they become a deadly combination, so deadly that once they were acted upon, the nature of a holy God could no longer have an affiliation with unholy man. Man's paradise was then ended, and for the first time, fear gained a beachhead in the mind of mankind. Fear has many companions, all of which were unintended consequences of a bad decision and none of which man was designed to cope with by his own strength. Man was and has continued to be separated relationally from his Creator. A rescue was needed, and that rescue was going to require a sacrifice.

God's first response to Adam and Eve's sin was to provide for them a covering of slain animal skins. However, that was only a temporary fix and would require ongoing blood sacrifices to keep the penalty of sin (which was death) at bay until a permanent solution was provided. All throughout the Old Testament there are prophetic utterances of a solution to man's death and discontinuity with God—over forty such prophecies written hundreds of years before God, in the person of Jesus, put on human flesh. The documentation of his birth is so irrefutable that it motivates Christians all over the world to celebrate that moment each year on the twenty-fifth day of December. Thirty-three years later that baby born on the first Christmas, now a grown man with divine credentials, paid the price that would redeem the lost relationship between God and man and bring them back together again.

It was at Calvary's cross where God sent his only son to redeem his prized possession. The chasm sin had created had become so great that man was not only separated from God, but the Bible tells us he had also become an enemy of God. Therefore, in a real sense, when Jesus left heaven for the purpose of redeeming mankind, he entered enemy territory. "For if, while we were God's enemies, we were reconciled to him through the death of his Son, how much more, having been reconciled, shall we be saved through his life (Rom. 5:10).

Man, once an enemy but now a child of God, not only has had his walk with God restored in the person of the Holy Spirit, but our Lord is now preparing a future home for us where we will live with Him for all eternity.

Day 19:

THE LOVE OF GOD
WAS EXPRESSED THERE

"For God so loved the world that he gave his one and only Son, that whosoever believes in him shall not perish but have eternal life" (John 3:16 NIV). There is probably no scripture better known or more often memorized than this one. It shows up on billboards and road signs and now, not so indiscriminately, on television during major sporting events. Nothing could be more profoundly expressed in its simplicity than John 3:16. This verse, above all others, is etched in the memory of people all over the world.

Yet as popular and well known as this verse may be, we often miss the depth of God's love and its significance. Fredrick Lehman, writer of the song "The Love of God" in 1919, may have gotten as close as anyone when he wrote, "Could we with ink the ocean fill and were the skies of parchment made, were every stalk on earth a quill and every man a scribe by trade, to write the love of God above would drain the ocean dry, nor could the scroll contain the whole though stretched from sky to sky"(from Fredrick Lehman's song "The Love of God").

As humans, we may never fully understand in this life what the Father and Son experienced in the giving process on the cross. The humiliation, the beatings, the lacerations, the crowning with thorns, the separation of bones, the piercing of hands and feet, the sword in the side, and the ultimate suffocation and painful death all describe the agony of the cross. The brutality of the cross and what Jesus suffered changed his features to the point of being unrecognizable: "His appearance was so disfigured beyond that of any human being and his form marred beyond human likeness" (Isa. 52:14 NIV). As terrible a description of the physical suffering of our Savior, through which he remained conscious and aware of his pain and suffering, it does not describe the God-level suffering that, as humans, we cannot fathom.

Our fallen nature obliterates so much of the majesty and glory of God that even though we have experienced the new birth, we are still limited in our understanding and insight because our previous nature remains. When we try to fully comprehend God's holiness, getting there seems to leave us with the feeling of "not quite." Jesus, for the first time in all of eternity, took on the full weight, identity, and ownership of our sin, and it caused his father to turn away. It is the opinion of many, including this writer, that He turned away from the sin his Son was bearing on the cross, not the son himself. Jesus on the other hand, at that moment, was experiencing the feeling of abandonment of bearing the sins of the world. So much so that for the first time in recorded history he refers to God as God, not as Father, as was his common practice when he was addressing or speaking of Him. "My God, my God, why have you forsaken me" (Matt. 27:46). As cruel and brutal as the physical punishment of the cross must have been, it paled in comparison to the agony that Jesus and God the Father must have experienced in this unparalleled and within the human mind, incomprehensible moment.

Why go through this? Why suffer so much physical and emotional pain? Why go through the whole process of the cross, experiencing real pain and dying a real death and being put into a real grave?

It was and is love. Jesus and the Father were motivated by a love for their prized creation, you and me and all the rest of humanity.

Without this righteous act of the Father, all of humanity would have been eternally separated from God, which is referred to as the "Second death" (Rev. 2:11 NIV). There was never a moment in all eternity when the love of God was more elaborately expressed than when Jesus gave his life on the cross.

Day 20:

OUR ROBE OF RIGHTEOUSNESS WAS WOVEN THERE

O f all the amazing realities associated with the cross, perhaps the most astounding is the thought that any of us would be considered righteous simply by believing Jesus gave his life at Calvary, was buried, and three days later was raised fully alive. Why? Because when we take an honest, Holy-Sprit-inspired look at our lives, we realize we (and everyone else) at one time or another have been deeply ensnared in the morass of wickedness. It becomes even more expressly true when we realize a holy, righteous God is the standard by which we make the comparison.

Thankfully, ours is not a righteousness predicated on our human performance, even though our lives will most definitely reflect changes associated with our newly acquired nature of being born again. This new nature becomes a formal declaration before God alone that we have been made pure and holy. It is a level of holiness man cannot see or feel, for that matter. Faith is its activator, and though other people can see some changes, only God can see the purified perfection, a perfection that addresses the demands of righteous judgment as well as provides the purity necessary to be a member of God's family.

When we take our last breath of earthly air, we will meet God as either Judge or Father, and what we have done with the cross within the short span of our lives will be the ultimate determining factor. To have known the truth and rejected it leaves us condemned. "Whoever believes in him is not condemned, but whoever does not believe stands condemned already because they have not believed in the name of God's one and only Son" (John 3:18 NIV). That person inevitably meets God as judge. To accept the sacrifice Jesus made at the cross as one's offering to God for a life that comes woefully short of perfection means that all vestiges of sin have been taken away, leaving us covered with the Shekinah (holy presence of God). Robed in God's righteousness, man can now meet God as Father. "What does the Scripture say? 'Abraham believed in God, and it was counted to him as righteousness.' Now to the one who works, his wages are not counted as a gift but as his due. But to the one who does not work but believes in him who justifies the ungodly, his faith is counted as righteousness" (Rom. 4:3-5 NIV).

Metaphorically speaking, it was on the cross that Jesus became the Great Tailor and the Holy Spirit became the Great Haberdasher. For those whose wardrobe includes such a righteous garment, they are assured of this promise: "But as it is written, Eye hath not seen, nor ear heard, neither have entered into the heart of man, the things God hath prepared for them that love him. But God hath revealed them unto us by his Spirit: for the Spirit searcheth all things, yea, the deep things of God" (1 Cor. 2:9-10 KJV). As wonderful as these revelations are, those associated with heaven are not only beyond description but are also beyond the grasp of the human mind while still entrapped in this earthly body.

Wearing the robe of Jesus's righteousness will allow you to walk right into the presence of God without fear or embarrassment, both now and when your assignment on earth is complete and you meet your Father God face to face.

Day 21:

THE SEARCH FOR SATISFACTION ENDS THERE

M ostly I have used the second and third person to express my thoughts relating to the cross throughout the previous twenty devotions. For this final devotion, though, I am choosing to write my thoughts in first person simply because it seems to be the most appropriate way to express my heartfelt appreciation for the cross of Jesus Christ.

The search for satisfaction is not always complete at the moment of spiritual conversion or what Jesus called being "born again." In my own experience, there was a sense in which forgiveness and being made righteous provided a freshness of spirit to my soul, but I quickly discovered I had not lost my appetite for things that did not seem to belong in the life of a member of the family of God. However, I gratefully also realized when I indulged in those things that at one time brought me pleasure, whether in attitude or action, now brought a sense of disgust and guilt.

What was I to do with this newfound faith that seemed to experience resistance from the leftovers of a pre-Christian lifestyle? The Word of God became my refuge, and the trail it placed me on has always led me back to the cross. It was at the cross where I learned my life was no longer my own. "Do you not know that your bodies are the temples of the Holy Spirit, who is in you, whom you have received from God? You are not your own; you were bought at a price. Therefore, honor God with your bodies" (1 Cor. 6:19-20 NIV).

It is at the cross where I learned and am still learning to be content with whatever circumstances God leads me into. "I know what it is to be in need and I know what it is to have plenty. I have learned the secret of being content in every situation, whether well fed or hungry, whether living in plenty or in want. I can do all this through him who gives me strength" (Phil. 4:12-13 NIV). This life change is not one of making a few adjustments; no, the cross has provided me the means for an entirely new life. The Bible compares it to having been raised from the dead. "When you were dead in your sins and in the circumcising of your flesh, God made you alive with Christ. He forgave all your sins, having canceled the charge of our legal indebtedness, which stood against us and condemned us; he has taken it away, nailing it to the cross" (Col. 2:13-14 NIV). In these verses, Paul is speaking of a person's spirit that has been dead to God but has now been made alive to Him.

Once the reality of the cross has taken the rightful and lofty position it deserves in the heart of any person, there is nothing left but the cross in which they may rightfully boast. "May I never boast except in the cross of our Lord Jesus Christ, through which the world has been crucified to me, and I to the world" (Gal. 6:14 NIV). Its measure on both small and great is incalculable.

The Roman Emperor Constantine, who lived during the second and third century, is known to have led in the rebuilding of the city of Trier, Germany. Following his conversion to Christianity, tradition has it that Constantine placed a cross atop a high pillar in the center of the city and made the decree that no business could take place except in view of that cross. The pillar remains there today although the cross has long ago eroded away. As the city grew into a thriving metropolis, it's expanse made Constantine's decree impossible to maintain.

How different would the world be today if every believer would elevate the cross high in the center of their hearts and determine to live each day in its overreaching shadow? All clamoring for and clinging to things less substantial would lose their attraction, and our search for satisfaction would be complete.

POSTSCRIPT

I t is my desire, coupled with sincere prayer, that spending twenty-one days reading about the cross of Jesus Christ with both its richness and its clarity of purpose has caused an enlargement in your heart to want to know more of this amazing centerpiece of history. If you have read this as a believer, I hope it has stimulated life change relative to your Christian walk and has enlarged things about the cross you did not previously know. At a minimum, I pray it has bound you again to the glorious realities associated with Jesus's sacrifice. Now with the cross as the tapestry behind you, I pray it has given you a desire to tell someone your story and its connection to it.

If you have read this as one who has not yet determined to place your faith in Christ's finished work, the mere fact you have read it in its entirety indicates there is a search taking place in your heart to find the satisfaction referred to in day twenty-one. Your search can actually end today by simply expressing to God that you know you are unworthy to be a part of His family and that you now recognize that only Jesus's death on the cross can make you worthy. Ask Him to take control of your life, and even though you will not be perfect, tell Him of your desire to live for Him. I pray you have made the decision to place your faith in Jesus Christ, and if you have, my suggestion is you again read *Twenty-One Days at the Cross*. You will find there are things you missed, and it will now be more meaningful to you.

Alan Cockrell

CPSIA information can be obtained
at www.ICGtesting.com
Printed in the USA
FSHW012125200620
71368FS

9 781631 291364